THEORY AND PRACTICE OF DREAMS

A pilot's guide to professional and personal realization

Luca Vanossi

LUCA VANOSSI

To all those who bet their lives
on their dreams

3

FOREWORD

Among the numerous publications available on the subject of professional achievement, many of which made by valid coaching and work psychology experts, the following book wants to be a synthesis of the experience in the field of someone who, like the author, have thrown himself into the labyrinth that separates daily life from his dreams armed with great hopes and good will, managing, after a lot of effort, to get where he wanted.

In the various chapters, individual qualities, operating methods and choice criteria that can contribute to the achievement of one's own professional goals will be analyzed. We will discuss the most important problems with which one has inevitably to deal along the way, starting with that of understanding whether the job of our dreams really belongs to us or not. We will also evaluate how these problems can be addressed and what are the indications that can make us understand that we have ventured down the wrong path.

Special attention will always be paid to personal change, an aspect that necessarily accompanies every professional training course and that is probably the most important side effect related to it.

The book is intended both for beginners, as those who for the first time enter the world of work and professional training, and for those who instead, perhaps after years of experience in a specific work sector, want to give a new twist to their own life, professional or personal.
Coming to terms with one's dreams is an experience that, sooner or later, everyone has to deal with. Difficult? Certainly. Exciting? To say the least. Understanding how to make our wishes come true through the choice of a profession, is one of the key moments of our existence, one in which we can realize we are doing something very important for our life.

In an increasingly virtual world, thinking that it is possible to materialize our dreams and make them present in everyday reality can be a difficult thing. Yet dreams are precisely those seeds that, if made to sprout, can really transform an unsatisfactory present into everything we are looking for: the important thing is to never stop believing in them.

Enjoy the reading.

The author

CHAPTER ONE: WHO I AM, WHERE I COME FROM, WHAT I DO

It is not possible to speak of professional achievement without including references to one's personal fulfillment, which includes the history, education, interests and choices that led a person to embark on a working and existential journey. Everyone has different characteristics and inclinations that interact with each other, orienting him in life, and I think it can be meaningful to take a closer look at the real path taken by someone who feels quite satisfied with the choices he has made and the goals he has achieved in professional and, at least partially, existential terms. Sure, it could be very difficult to score a perfect hit, but it's possible to get close enough. Among the many stories of those who managed to get more or less exactly where they wanted, I would like to talk about one that I know pretty well: mine. Now, I certainly don't want to set myself as an example for others or to emphasize how good I was in getting to the end of a complex path, but only to share an experience that I am sure everyone can do, since I did it. Having once managed, with a small revolution, to change my life completely, I feel I can talk about it, thinking that someone will find it useful to know how my journey was and what are my reflections about it. So who am I and what is my story? I am an aircraft pilot and I fly on intercontinental routes. My work is very stimulating, even if at times tiring and difficult: on the one hand, it gives strong emotions and great satisfaction, on the other it requires study, application, good health, psychophysical balance and, above all, the ability to work in harmony with a group of people. I have not always been a pilot: although it has been a passion of mine for a long time, I started out as an engineer. My parents were both teachers, and in my family study and culture were something as inevitable and necessary as daily food. Attention to academic results was maximum and attending university, after high school, was an absolutely obvious and unquestionable fact. The nuclear engineering course was long and difficult, but very interesting. The years I spent at the faculty were a good time in my life, especially thanks to the good friends I was lucky enough to find (we still hang out). Why did I choose nuclear engineering? Because I had always liked physics and because I thought that that degree would almost force me to find work abroad, given that the chances of working in the field in Italy were scarce or non-existent. Going abroad: even then I understood that the work I could find in the future should preferably include this aspect. Apart from the profession itself, the possible lifestyle linked to it also had its own importance. Starting university courses, I soon realized something else: of the thirty exams required for graduation, almost all consisting of a written and an oral test, less than half were directly concerned what I had come to study. The rest was related to subjects that I did not like at all, but that it was still necessary to learn in order to be able to deal with what really interested me. It wasn't easy. Even after graduation, the impact with the labour market was very complicated: not that there were no opportunities, but it was almost impossible to find a job that had to do with what I had studied for so long. I still needed a salary so I started sending out resumes, and I was invited to several interviews. I was offered jobs which I honestly found almost impossible to do. Once, for example, I was contacted by a large company in the industrial hinterland of my town, part of an international group. They didn't tell me exactly what they were offering me: they had got my name from the Alumni Association of my university and they would have liked to meet and talk to me. On a rainy November day, I took the car and drove for an hour and a half, slowly advancing through the traffic of the ring road, finally arriving at the former steel mill that housed the offices and laboratories. I showed up at the reception and, shortly after, a sad-looking girl dressed in grey took me to her boss, in a dimly lit study full of technical books. After introducing himself, the engineer asked me a few questions and took me to see the laboratories where, proudly showing me a group of machines that twisted pieces of metal, he explained to me what the job consisted of: subjecting the components of mechanical parts belonging to structures involved in accidents to different types of loads. This would have made it possible to determine the cause of their rupture under stress. "It's an important job," he explained to me, "and doing it right requires thorough preparation: if we were to hire you, you'll spend the first six months studying almost every book you've seen in my office". As a final test, the engineer submitted to me a problem of mechanics applied to machines, telling me that I had five minutes to solve it and explain how I had done it. Not being a person who likes to leave things unfinished, I solved the problem and stayed for the last part of the interview. I was told that it was a two-year job training contract that provided for only an extremely low flat rate reimbursement for the first year, but that the precious offer would have allowed me to gain an experience that would help me to continue my career dedicated to the study of ruptures under stress. I was speechless and, to be honest, also breathless. I thanked them for their time and their kindness, but told them that I was not interested in that job, leaving them stunned. While I was slowly coming back home, I was on the verge of despair: I had studied beautiful and interesting topics and, nevertheless, I only found proposals for alienating jobs. What did the future hold for me? Having to compromise, I accepted a job in the IT sector of a water treatment company that also produced desalinators for boats: I didn't care much about the job, and the salary was still low, but at least I had the chance to go to some seaside resort and visit amazing yachts to make the necessary installations. I also switched to the sales management sector to have more opportunities to move and stay outside Italy. I became more and more aware of how much the idea of traveling was constantly present in guiding my choices. In the meantime, I had met flight attendants who introduced me to pilots, and so I had the opportunity to get to know their work and their way of life more closely: I was very impressed. Flying had always been a hidden desire of mine and I had spent half of my childhood building model airplanes, fantasizing about piloting them and flying them in the sky. I had imagined myself traveling the world hundreds of times, piloting one of those wonders, but there was a little problem: I had never really believed in it. Studying, graduating, attending university: this was what I had absorbed from my family. They were good things, no doubt about it, but the result did not satisfy me. I kept on thinking about the pilots' job: I tried to talk to some of them again and to retrieve as much information as I could. This thing was getting more and more attractive. One day I was working in Monte Carlo and I was returning to the city after having supervised the installation of a desalinator on a beautiful boat moored at the port of Fontvieille. I had to work the next day too, and the customer was paying for a nice hotel. As I was entering the hall, I saw a billboard advertising the next Formula One Grand Prix, which was to be held shortly thereafter. In the image a driver was speeding by on a wonderful single-seater and a writing in English read: "Some men do what others dream of". The slogan struck me, and that phrase began to spin in my brain. The months passed and for the Christmas holidays I went on vacation to Mexico with an hostess friend. Again, I lived two weeks in close contact with the flight crew, seeing how they lived and worked, asking questions and getting answers. Their work was basically made up of study, technical skills, and travel: not bad. There was certainly a lot of effort, even physical, but it seemed a small price to pay to be able to do something really stimulating and get out of the gray routine that the jobs I had found offered. Those were two decisive weeks: I thought about it, did the math and put on the scales the countless question marks that lay in front of me, on the one hand, together with the powerful enthusiasm that filled my heart, on the other. I decided that it was worth the risk, and after a few months spent organizing myself with finances, I quit my job and left for the United States, determined to become a pilot. Almost everyone believed I was crazy: quitting a steady job, ditching a girlfriend, spending a lot of money that I could have used to buy a house were not things that many could understand. My enthusiasm might have been sky-high, but a road full of uncertainties was opening up before me. I had never really flown, I didn't know what it meant, maybe I wouldn't have liked it. Also, once I got the license, would I also get a job? It was something very unclear and the answers I received about it were vague. However two reasons pushed me to go on: the first was that whatever I would have found at the end of my journey would still be better than the reductive and unsatisfactory existence I had before; the second that, after a long time, I finally felt alive, and my life had once again begun to make sense. I started the course and found that I liked flying. Of course it was a very different type of flight than the one I was used to as a passenger: it was mostly exercises and maneuvers on small propeller airplanes. It was not easy at all, I had many moments of despair and often I wondered if I had taken the wrong path. What kept pushing me forward were the good results I was getting, the new life I found myself living and, above all, the two reasons mentioned above. Even though I was still far from the goal, I found that even just changing direction and taking a new path that I liked was something that gave my life much more meaning than what I previously did. One year later I was a commercial pilot: I still had some time left on my J1 Visa, and eventually I found a way to fly some more time. By chance I came to know a guy who owned a boat charter company operating between the United States and the Bahamas. The company had several yachts and some airplanes with which they transferred passengers directly to the islands where their boats were located. I asked him if I could give a hand, and he accepted: it was for free, but it was a wonderful opportunity to build up flying hours. I stayed in Florida for another eight months, taking tourists to those beautiful places: I was making no money, but I was happy with what I was doing. When the Visa expired, I returned to Italy where I started the conversion procedures for the Italian flight license, earning a living by teaching mathematics, physics and aeronautical subjects in various high schools. Once a month I took the car and went to all the airlines offices in the northern part of the country, where I lived, personally introducing myself to hand over a resume and asking to speak with the chief pilot. I succeeded only a few times, but I noticed that my resourcefulness, along with my university degree, was appreciated. However I did not lose heart and went on month after month, in the meantime sending spontaneous applications to many other airlines. After almost a year, in an absolutely unexpected way, two of the companies called me one after the other to invite me to a selection. Commitment aside, I was also lucky: in aviation there are periods of stasis, where it's almost impossible to find a job, that alternate with periods of extreme need, and I had just come across one of these. I had to pass the selection though, and in an airline that's not just an interview. It usually starts with a series of logic-mathematical tests followed by technical questions about aero-technics, aircraft systems and aeronautical regulations. It continues with other English language tests and, above all, psychological tests and interviews. Then there is a check on the flight simulator, where maneuvers in normal and emergency conditions are analyzed, with the candidate often finding himself piloting an unknown aircraft model for the first time. After an airline medical check, finally the survivors have an interview with the Chief Pilot and the Director of Personnel. It usually takes at least two or three days to complete everything. Both went well: I had studied a lot and worked hard, never stopping training even when I wasn't flying. I received a job offer from the two airlines, chose the one that seemed the best and I was sent to France for a course on my first jet aircraft. After two very busy months, I achieved my first 'Type Rating' on an Airbus A320. I returned to Italy and began the standardization training, for the airline's specific procedures, doing about twenty routes and a final flight check. I was qualified for the company, but not yet for the Italian state: to obtain the airline pilot license, I had to wait until I got fifteen hundred flight hours and other exams with the national aeronautical authorities. After about two years I obtained my airline pilot's license. The journey had been long and demanding, but very stimulating. However, studying and training were certainly not finished: the professional life of a pilot is dotted with periodic examinations, including medical ones, and with long and demanding simulator sessions, not to mention the need to keep constantly up to date with the continuous changes of the aeronautical regulations in different parts of the world. There are international criteria that identify the minimum levels of skills, scores and physical state necessary to be able to continue to carry out the profession, and if they are not met one is "grounded", meaning that it is no longer possible to fly. Despite the complexity of my new profession, I was very happy with what I was doing: it was my job now, and it involved me completely. After two years I was moved to intercontinental flights and my life, professional and otherwise, became exactly how I wanted it. It was very varied, interesting and full of novelties: of course sometimes it was demanding, especially from a physical point of view, but it was just what I was looking for. Over time the disadvantages related to one's work tend to become more evident and, indeed, due to a mysterious spread of the second law of thermodynamics in everyday life, they usually include precisely those aspects that one would most like to avoid. However, in retrospect, I can say that I am really satisfied with how things went and happy to have worked hard to reach my goal. The happiness that follows fatigue is one of the most beautiful emotions you can feel in life. The relationship with myself has also changed, improving: everything I went through to get to where I am now has made me more confident, more prepared to face the unexpected, more open and able to communicate with others and more grateful to life for all that it can offer me. This is, in short, the story of my professional change. I would like to avoid adding any personal comment at present, leaving to the readers the opportunity to carry out their own analysis and to identify those critical issues, strengths, resources, decision-making criteria, working methods and personal qualities that may have helped me to achieve my goals. This could give everyone the chance to draw a sort of personal 'road map' that leads to the realization of their desires.

CHAPTER TWO: HORIZONS AND COMPASSES

If we want to go somewhere, first of all we need a destination: we must know where to go, and the same happens when it comes to our professions. It's essential to become aware of what we really like so that we can draw a first line that connects the condition in which we are to the one we want to arrive at, in order to define a path that we can follow later. It may seem trivial, but actually it's not easy at all: when it comes to making professional choices there are many who don't know exactly what to do, and the reasons can be many. For example, there are those who think they have no real passion: for these people choosing a job is often something hazy and random, a choice made without a guiding criterion that could help them in the chaotic sea of different opportunities. The many possible choices confuse them, making their decisions and the definition of their priorities difficult. Others have a passion, but they don't believe in it enough, and in the end they let it be stifled by other considerations, apparently more concrete and 'safe'. These two risky conditions can lead to a huge waste of time or to work situations that gradually become alienating, if they are not balanced by other values in one's life. Probably the most success-ful people are those who have a passion in life and try to follow it, making it their profession, or those who know the reasons why they want to do a certain job. In fact, it is not only *passions* that provide valid reasons capable of attracting a person to their work goal: there are other *motivations* that can play an equally powerful and crucial role in pushing each of us towards a professional ob-jective. Let's think, for example, of *money* or *career*: these are con-cepts that we can hardly define 'passions', but which continue to deeply motivate many people, allowing them to compensate for the effort made to achieve a certain professional position (often a lot) through rewards like having more money, more power or more personal prestige. Even *challenge* can be a motivation to undertake particularly demanding paths: for many people this is in fact the main reason, and the harder the route the more they feel they are doing something that is worth their efforts. Often people motivated by challenge can excel in many fields, but they risk never finding their own definitive professional position, bouncing from one job to another or from one responsibility to another without ever truly appreciating what they have done or where they got to. *Money*, *career* and *challenge* are undoubtedly very powerful *motivations*, but if taken individually and in an absolute sense they can lead to conditions of particular psychophysical stress, given that the profession that generates them as by-products is often not pleasant in itself, but precisely because it can provide these things. *Peace of mind* can also be a motivation (we will talk more about it in a later chapter): there are those who choose a job because it will not take too much from them, leaving more space for other pleasant aspects of their life, or because - not being a particularly complex one- will not generate high stress levels. This usually collides with the reasons discussed above, whereby easier professions usually give less chance of having money, careers, challenges and everything associated with them. Naturally, these are just some generic examples: there are countless reasons that can effectively push people towards a given professional goal, motivating them and guiding them effectively. In the meantime, starting from these considerations, we can make some preliminary reflections. The first is that, probably, those who have a passion or a strong motivation will have a better chance of achieving a satisfying profession than those who do not. In fact, the latter are lacking not only an effective beacon that can illuminate the path they are taking, but also a possible support that allows them to face more effectively the inevitable difficulties they will encounter. The second consideration is that passions and motivations can act not only independently but also in synergy, complementing and amplifying each other. As for my personal experience, the choice to become a pilot had the advantage of bringing together different passions and motivations, equally important at different levels: the opportunity to travel, to carry out a demanding but very rewarding technical job, to work in teams with different people of various nationalities, to operate in different parts of the world, to earn well, to visit many countries but, at the same time, to have quality free time (when not flying, a pilot is completely free from work, even mentally, for whole days), etc. Each of these individual aspects was very interesting and attractive to me, but perhaps not important enough to be, on its own, sufficient to project myself with certainty towards a given profession. It was the search and identification of a type of work that could best bring together all these instances that allowed me in the end to say clearly: 'I want to do this'. This, of course, implies that the passions and motivations, surely important if not fundamental, are not by themselves sufficient to carry us to the end of the professional path: qualities and, above all, commitment are necessary. We will come back to talk about this, more specifically, later. A further reflection, taking into account what has been said so far, leads to the importance of a principle that constitutes, in my opinion, the fundamental basis for successfully identifying a valid professional path (and not only): an *honest personal analysis*. I believe the first step towards our dream job is to understand who we are and how we are. It's not immediate: we have all developed, over time, a series of beliefs or prejudices towards ourselves, others and the world, which can lead us to see the reality to which we belong in a distorted or even untruthful way. The causes of all this are many, not least the continuous messages with which the world, the society, and even the people closest to us, perhaps thinking to lend a hand, continue to send us, presenting stereotypes which are almost mandatory for a successful personal, social and professional life. This can plunge us into a state of confusion that can further compromise the chance of making a winning decision for our future, especially if we experience a contrast between what we feel inside and what is offered to us from the outside. The most effective solution, in my opinion, is to look inside ourselves, leaving out what doesn't belong to us, understanding with curiosity, sincerity and humility who we really are. It's a long process, certainly not a quick exercise that can be done by thinking about it from time to time for a few minutes. It's something that must be sought seriously, quietly and, perhaps, considering that many of the things that we have come to take for granted about our present and future life may actually be comfortable but fake screens. Only by looking seriously inside ourselves will it be possible to see the traces of those passions, interests, motivations, desires, enthusiasms, dislikes, skills and availability that will allow us to evaluate with greater awareness the various professional choices that will open up before us. What does it mean to consciously evaluate a professional option? It means identifying it as attractive, placing it within our possibilities and evaluating, as far as possible, the pros and cons. This does not always happen, especially if we consider the case of those who, struggling to find their own passions or motivations, abandon themselves to models offered by others. An example can be that of the new professions generated by the spread of social media. Many young people today want to become a successful influencer or blogger, getting rich and famous in a short time: the fundamental requirement is to have many followers. The problem lies in the fact that it's not very clear how one can manage to be followed by thousands or millions of people. The vast majority of those who try this path do so by counting on chance, since someone has succeeded simply by posting photos or videos of dances, daily life, exotic landscapes, sculptural bodies or Zen quotes. It's a bit the fulfillment, in a broad sense, of Warhol's prophecy of "fifteen minutes of fame for everyone": it's not required to know how to do something, you just need to appear on a screen and maybe, by some unknown mechanism, success will take you far away. Is there any kind of awareness in a choice like this? I would say no: you notice the advantages, you work mechanically, but you don't really know what you are doing. Still remaining in this area, it is different when someone becomes a successful blogger or influencer because he has first learned to do something interesting and particular, and for this very reason he is followed by people. An example very close to me is that of a friend, a violinist, who, following her passion and after studying and working hard for a long time, has become very famous, so a lot of people started following her on social media. Over time several stylists and jewelers have ended up turning to her to advertise their products on her social media, also making her become a successful influencer. The same thing happens to actors, musicians, sportsmen, writers, scientists, artisans and so on: they have many followers because they did something before landing on social networks. They have something of their own to offer, a passion to share. A little different, right? It may well be that someone still manages to become an influencer by chance, posting hundreds of dances, photos or quotes of the day, but what are the chances that this will happen? We can therefore understand the power of a conscious professional choice. One of the best consequences of this type of approach lies in the fact that it allows us to more effectively compare our expectations with the real world, also allowing us to begin to glimpse the shape of the path that we must follow to reach our goals. In order to be able to make a judgment that is as complete as possible, it's also necessary to obtain a lot of information about what we want to do. Often people tend to have a partial and sometimes preconceived view on many aspects of life, including work, ending up grasping only the most attractive parts of a given profession. Having a more complete picture can certainly increase the degree of awareness with which you decide to tackle a career path. This may also include an analysis of the *supply and demand* for a particular job: knowing how much a job position is in demand or not, can give us a clearer vision of what we can expect in the future. What, on the other hand, is possible to do if we cannot find clear passions or strong motivations in ourselves? I believe that it's always necessary to identify at least small traces that tell us about what we like or dislike, and it will be precisely by putting them all together that we will at least be able to get an idea of - *if not exactly where we want to go - at least where we don't want to*, and then act accordingly. For each possible choice we will find pros and cons, and by weighing them we will be able to see which side the scales tip for each career path taken into consideration. What if, during this process, we realize that, under the lens of our critical conscience, our passions collide with other motivations? What to do, for example, if we are very attracted to a given profession but we already know it will make us earn very little? Once again, extreme honesty with ourselves is required to be able to make an effective decision. By drawing on my experience and that of several people whom I have dealt with, I believe that in the long run following the path shown by a passion is more rewarding and fulfilling than taking the one indicated by a motivation. I have often noticed that people who are happier for the work they do are also generally more serene in their life, and tend to better deal with any other 'shortcomings' or sacrifices related to their career choice than those who are supported by financial rewards. In the long run, the latter are more likely to end up perceiving daily work only as a sacrifice, perhaps necessary but unpleasant and insignificant for their realization, and this can lead to critical situations, from a personal point of view. Finally it's very important, especially if you are looking at the topic of professional choice for the first time, to *talk* and *discuss* with those who already have an experience in this sense and can give you clearer ideas about the world of work or how much money, career, commitment and free time can be important for your future life. In this sense, parents are generally the most obvious and available resource for a young person, and often, precisely because they are genuinely interested in their children's future, they may be able to emphasize some of the most salient or critical aspects relating to a possible professional choice. We must say, however, that sometimes, even if moved by a real interest and desire to do well, they can fall into the trap of wanting to push their children towards goals that perhaps belong more to themselves, not really paying attention to inclinations and desires, which may be a little unclear, of those in front of them. Sometimes it happens that they too do not have the necessary or sufficient information to effectively guide their sons towards an effective career choice. Perhaps it would be desirable that parents could accompany them along the path of their professional choice without any presumption, helping them, through their work and life experience, to smooth out the gaps and perplexities they may face when deciding which path to take. Sometimes it happens that they too do not have the necessary or sufficient information to effectively guide their sons towards an effective career choice. Of course there are also other important figures to whom it is possible to turn to for information, to ask for advice or to express doubts: first of all are the teachers, who sometimes know even better than the parents themselves, thanks to their work, about the inclinations and interests of a youngster. I believe that proper communication between parents and teachers is crucial to make available new opinions that can be truly effective for someone's career guidance. If we are trying to find confirmation of our aspirations, a way to our dreams or simply a trace towards our future profession, a good thing to do is to ask to parents, teachers or people who have experience in the field: they may know us very well and certainly they have already gone through the same kind of problems. The final decision will remain ours, but we will have a team of people from whom we can draw valuable information that can help us. In fact we must not forget that every profession, starting from its origin, is never something that comes entirely from a solitary effort, but necessarily needs interaction with others. The so-called team work is crucial, and it's possible to use it to our advantage even when it comes to understanding what work to do. Each of us depends on other people more than we think, and the whole world of work, from training onwards, revolves more and more around cooperation. At school, or more generally during training, we realize how important interpersonal interactions are, not only those with teachers but also those with our classmates and friends, with whom we discuss, share efforts and often help each other, working together. In this sense the training structures are also part of the network that can provide effective support to career guidance, and among the various opportunities offered for comparison we can mention the meetings with professionals from various sectors who, speaking of their work, can offer clear examples of what it means to undertake a given career path. Other figures, such as psychologists, coaches or labor experts, are also increasingly involved in initiatives related to career guidance and can provide information on a person's potential professional inclinations.

CHAPTER THREE: WHAT TO PACK

So, by confronting ourselves we found passions, motivations, or other reasons that showed us where we really want to go. The haze is gone and the light is shining on the road to our goal, illuminating it almost completely. Now what? Now it's time to look at this road very carefully, trying to figure out what it looks like up close, how long it is, if there are any uphill sections and what's hiding in the dark corners. In the beginning every path seems quite clear and linear, although maybe not simple, and once again it takes a very serious and honest approach to be able to understand if it's really so or if what is in front of us is quite different from what, at first glance, we might expect. Before asking ourselves what we need to start the journey, we need to understand *if we really want to do it*. In fact it may be that, although we have identified a profession that attracts us, we realize that the path necessary to get there is difficult for us, fraught with uncertainty, or simply very long. Looking inside ourselves, as well as helping us to identify passions and motivations, can also make us understand how much we are really willing to dedicate ourselves and to work to get where we want to be. That said, we certainly do not want to urge the reader to immediately desist from choosing a given career path if by chance he or she should see some difficulties, certain or hypothetical: generally, the bigger the dreams, the more effort it takes to make them come true, but the most difficult things are also the most rewarding, and the relative path is the most stimulating and meaningful for one's own fulfillment. It is good to evaluate things knowing that making a little effort beforehand, trying to get where you want to go, means not only being happier afterwards, but also avoiding the risk of running into a tiring working future because you are locked into the narrow and uncomfortable world of a profession that you don't like. Taking into account what has been said so far, my first piece of advice is to find out as much information as possible about the training path you plan to undertake, by talking to someone who has already done so. People are always the first resource at our disposal, and often, as well as answering questions, they can also give us something more, showing us points of view that we might never have imagined. Feel free to talk to others, and remember that usually people like it when someone shows interest in what they do or know. Often schools provide tools that allow you to obtain valuable information on career guidance, and of course this also includes the related training path. Once in possession of all the information that we have been able to collect, we will be able to make a more informed choice about *our willingness* to take a given path, although we will probably realize that some aspects of what awaits us will continue to remain foggy. There will still be some shadow areas that, no matter how hard we try, we will not be able to fully illuminate: the *risks*. Risks are part of everyone's daily life and can never be completely erased. What can be done is to *reduce their size*: if we have carefully considered a possible goal, looking inside it honestly, evaluating ourselves well, and obtaining all possible information, we have done everything to reduce the risk associated with our choice, and we can move forward with a clear conscience. In any case it must be emphasized that even after having acted in the best possible way to maximize the chances of success of our decision, we will still not have the *certainty* of being able to fully achieve our professional goal. How can we face this criticality? Before expressing my opinion, I would like to cite an example that I believe to be very significant about the attitude of some, or perhaps many, towards the uncertainty that inevitably accompanies every type of choice in life, and in this case, the professional one. A friend psychologist I recently had the opportunity to talk to, told me that he attended a meeting between the Italian astronaut Paolo Nespoli and the students of a high school, organized by the institute itself for professional orientation purposes. Mr. Nespoli told the students that in his path to become an astronaut, in addition to graduation, specialization, work and selections, he also had to train and stay updated for a good ten years before being chosen for a mission. A boy, raising his hand, asked him, a little incredulous: "Yes, but you knew that in the end they would offer you a mission, right?". The answer was "No": Nespoli had no certainty that after all those years of study, training and hard work he would participate in a mission, yet he continued, he went on and, in the end, after so much time and so much effort, he fulfilled his dream of going into space. Uncertainty is the daily bread of every profession, even more so if it is a fascinating one, but you have to know how to accept and manage it in order to eventually get somewhere. My opinion in this regard echoes the example given by Nespoli to those boys: *commit yourself and go on*. It is worthwhile to face uncertainties, risks and hardships in order to have the opportunity to make your wishes come true. In any case, while it is true that difficulties should not be underestimated, it's also true that we should not overestimate them or devalue ourselves: generally a person can manage to get where he wants, if he is well motivated and has no obvious material limitations. And what if you had to commit and work hard but couldn't reach the goal? We will have the opportunity to talk about it later: for now, suffice it to say that even just walking the road that leads to our dreams will give us something great that we did not have in us before. Now let's analyze which inner resources are useful to face the path that opens up before us. The first is undoubtedly a natural *inclination* towards something that has to do with a certain profession. Someone likes science, someone loves Greek and Latin, another one loves sports or music, and each of them does each of these things well. It may be, therefore, that by tapping into our personal abilities it is easier to slide towards professions that include what we like and what we do best: let yourself go. Someone will tell us to consider the pros and cons of a choice of this kind that is sometimes 'easier' precisely because it's guided by our predispositions, but let's remember that in the end it will be us, not the others, who will have to live with our job for a long time. Dealing with something that we do well will undoubtedly facilitate us along the way, will make what we do pleasant and will allow us to take off part of the inevitable weight of the training path, also allowing us to have more time to devote to those parts that can be more complex. Another important and, I would say, fundamental tool to advance along our route is a *study or work method*. Having a method allows us to better manage our forces, directing them more effectively towards what we find ourselves facing from time to time. A good method allows us to optimize the *time* we dedicate to training, since it is often limited by other, necessary, daily needs. It should be remembered, in fact, that it's not only the *quantity* of the commitment we put into what we do that makes our action more effective, but above all the *quality* linked to how we do it. Studying and staying really focused on a subject for two hours and then going for sports or recreation, is usually much more useful than spending the whole day on books without really absorbing something, tiring the mind and not giving it an opportunity to recover. A method is something that we will carry with us for the rest of our lives, a very useful tool that we will have forged and perfected over time and that will remain at our disposal whenever we need it. Often, with few variations, we will then be able to adapt the study method by transforming it into a working one, and it's undeniable that reaching one's profession having already developed a good organizational capacity is a great advantage. As with other qualities, not all people have a natural tendency to give rise to a methodology in dealing with the daily commitments of their existence. Nevertheless having a method is really necessary to advance, and it's possible to start creating it simply by experimenting with different ways of organizing, progressively identifying what, in your opinion, works best for you. It should also be remembered that since a method is something very personal, adopting the one proposed by others may not work: perhaps it could be a starting point, but later it will be necessary to structure one's own. The third tool that I would like to propose is a behavioral attitude: knowing how to balance the attention we turn to the difficulties as they arise, reminding us of our goal. This may seem trivial, but I think it's very important. If we fail to focus on what we are doing *now* we cannot move forward, while if we do not look at our *goal* from time to time we risk losing the *sense* of what we are doing, making our efforts even heavier. Knowing how to manage these two aspects, without forgetting one or the other, can help us to continue in a better way. A resource that will never miss along our path is *people*. In addition to being useful for identifying our goals and giving us information, they can play a crucial role, even during the training period and the subsequent employment, sometimes becoming decisive for our success. They can help, support and advise us while we are learning and direct, guide and sponsor us while we're about to enter the work market. I can say that in most cases if someone is able to lend a hand he will gladly do it: maybe he will not be able to do that much, but he will try to help us as much as he can. It's pleasant, and sometimes surprising, to find this beautiful form of solidarity between people: after all everyone has struggled to get a job, and everyone feels close to those who find themselves living what they have previously experienced, knowing how important it is to have someone by your side. Using the resources that people make available to us simply means being open and talking to them about our needs, knowing that they will gladly give a hand. This is also true in the workplace: a clear and open attitude certainly allows us to create a more efficient, functional and harmonious working environment: here is, once again, a tool that will not only be useful during our training course, but whose usefulness will always last. The ability to manage one's relationships with others, even within a horizon aimed at professional achievement, is one of the qualities that belong to a group of very important personal resources that make up what is defined as *emotional intelligence*. The concept of emotional intelligence is complex, interesting and very important: I recommend everyone to read Daniel Goleman's book about it to be able to deepen its meaning and begin to better develop the great resources that we unknowingly carry within. The qualities that fall within the sphere of emotional intelligence are many and all very significant, also from a professional point of view. In fact, I believe that they are by far the most important when it comes to managing our life in the best possible way, including the professional choices. What are the most relevant personal resources, from an emotional point of view, that we can use, identifying and cultivating them in us? I believe that the first is *tenacity*, that is the ability to hold on and not give up in the face of adversity that we may encounter along the way. It has been demonstrated that successful people, those who in various fields come to fulfill their professional dreams, are not the smartest or the most gifted, but those who manage not to be discouraged by difficulties and unexpected events, however great they may be. If they fall they get up and continue, or they have a plan B ready for use. These individuals will be statistically more successful in life, and also in their job. Another tool is *patience*, that is the ability to know how to postpone personal gratification over time: normally we all want to see the results of our efforts as soon as possible, we want to feel good 'immediately'. However this is almost impossible if we find ourselves chasing a dream, perhaps a very complex one, and therefore we must be able to manage a long period of efforts that, in some moments, will seem to never end, without even being sure of if or when we will be able to reap something of what we are painstakingly sowing. A part of us will always try to push us to give up everything, to make us leave a path that presents many sacrifices and few satisfactions: it's a sort of self-defense mechanism that aims to stop a process that is perceived as painful or harmful. Those who manage to be patient, shifting the need for gratification forward, are able to proceed and arrive at previously unimaginable states of personal satisfaction. It must also be said that the amount of effort required by a given training path is largely subjective, and often the perception of the relative fatigue is amplified by our common lack of objectivity. It may be that things are not so difficult after all and perhaps there are positive aspects in the path we are taking: rather than a heap of difficult commitments, perhaps it's a beautiful and exciting adventure. Another quality to consider is *empathy*, that is the ability to intercept the moods of other people and understand them. Recalling what we said a little while ago about the importance that human relationships have, both in terms of training and work, we can well understand how empathy is an absolutely necessary resource for those facing a professional journey. Lastly, among the many that emotional intelligence includes, I would like to mention two other truly fundamental qualities, also useful in everyday life: *optimism* and *self-confidence*. Without them the path to a goal of any kind would become really impossible. We all carry inside each of these qualities, even if they emerge differently in each of us. The secret to make them available is to *cultivate* them, that is to make them emerge through one's behavior. One can become more empathetic by being more open and available with others, more tenacious by not giving up in the hardest moments, more optimistic by refusing to fall into reductive visions of oneself and the future. As for self-confidence, it is precisely by continuing to advance, by learning from one's mistakes, that it is possible to make it grow. Taking the road that leads to our dreams, even without having reached our destination, is already giving us new and great opportunities. Developing the qualities useful for our future profession is a kind of training that can help add something new and beautiful to who we are.

CHAPTER FOUR: OBSTACLE RACING

Once we have embarked on the path towards our goal, even after minimizing the risks in every way and carefully placing the resources that may be useful in our backpack, it can happen, as it often does in life, to find ourselves in front of a series of unexpected *obstacles*. More than possibilities we can speak of certainties, especially when it comes to professional achievement: we already mentioned, in the first chapter, that mysterious phenomenon relating to the propagation of the second principle of thermodynamics in our existence for which every human activity, in addition to bringing with itself the desired purposes, it is also bound to generate unexpected problems. It may well be that, although inevitable, the obstacles that we may find in our way are not exactly great: perhaps they could be more similar to difficult experiences than to substantial problems. However we must consider that the boundary that separates the ways of perceiving the same problem is purely subjective, and what someone sees only as a stone could seem to another a boulder, and vice versa. I have never met anyone, myself included, who at a certain point in their training or career did not ask themselves: "Did I take the wrong path?". It has happened almost to everyone, and those who did not have this doubt still had to measure themselves with difficulties that at times really seemed to definitively block the way to their dreams. How to deal with all this? What answers can we give to our doubts and how can we find them? First of all, a good thing to do is to bring the obstacle facing us back to a *different perspective*, so that we can better understand what its true dimensions are. It's good to learn to *relativize* the problems we are encountering, changing the curvature of the mental lens with which we analyze what happens to us, knowing that often the common tendency is to *amplify* the proportions of what we find difficult. From another perspective, perhaps a more realistic one, what previously seemed an insurmountable mountain may simply turn out to be a hill, perhaps a little higher than usual, but one that we can certainly cross with a change of pace. Let's not forget that obstacles are a constant in life, and therefore it may be a good idea to *start learning to overcome* them; their appearance on our path, professional or existential, can provide us with an important opportunity to train ourselves to develop skills that will serve us in many situations for the rest of our lives. To change the perspective with which we perceive an obstacle, we can also imagine acting in two complementary ways: doing work on ourselves and asking others for help. In the first case we will try to find the right level of objectivity that can allow us to evaluate the problem we are facing with greater equilibrium; in the second case we can instead refer to other people, to someone we trust, looking for other points of view, talking, discussing, asking for opinions and support. Of course we can think of doing both, but when the obstacle is more formal than substantial, perhaps a personal analysis will be sufficient. Once again, looking within ourselves with honesty can change things, and we must remember that being honest with ourselves also means knowing how to recognize our abilities and re-evaluate ourselves. Comparing with others, on the other hand, becomes indispensable if we think that what we are facing is a complex structural problem and not a specific difficulty such as, for example, that of not being able to pass an exam that is particularly difficult or unwelcome. A more serious problem can instead occur if everything we are doing seems meaningless, uninteresting or really too heavy: in this case it is certainly better to talk to someone. This can make a difference, and often the opinion of a person we respect can lead us to change our minds about a situation that seemed apparently hopeless. Apart from the fact that those who listen to us may have already gone through what we are experiencing, and therefore are able to offer us the example of their direct experience, even the mere act of sharing our problems with others is often the first step towards their resolution. Seeking the opinion of another person means taking a different approach to our difficulties. Maybe someone will really be able to reassure us, giving us a meaningful opinion or showing us a way out, but even if this were not the case we might realize that we have implicitly acted in order to relativize the obstacle that we have to face. This often results into regaining greater self-confidence and therefore feeling more able to dominate the problem and overcome it, or to be able to find other ways that allow us to get around the obstacle and reach our goal in another way. In fact it isn't always necessary to remove what can prevent us from continuing: sometimes we can use our emotional intelligence and our other abilities to find alternative solutions. As a pilot, I would like to share a technique that I learned during training, which is summarized in an acronym that traces an ideal decision-making path to follow during an emergency on board: I think it can provide a clear indication of how to organize a mental process that would allow to effectively manage any type of problem. As we know accidents can happen during the flight, and they can escalate into very critical situations. Moreover, given the complexity of the systems, it's sometimes difficult to understand, among the many information that comes to the attention of the pilots, what exactly the problem is. The risk, in these cases, is to end up in a 'tunnel vision' situation, where the ability to maintain an open and objective view of what is happening is lost. Finally, since in the meantime the airplane continues to move quickly, the time to make an effective decision is limited. Keeping in mind that the last decision-maker on board, the commander, will work with his team to deal with the situation, evaluating information, asking for opinions, accepting advice, setting priorities and distributing tasks, he will finally refer to a sort of mental road map condensed into an acronym (*FORDER*) that will allow him to follow an effective path to tackle the problem in the best possible way. *FORDER* stands for *Facts, Options, Risks and benefits, Decision, Execution, Review*: the idea is that, by following the indications given by the individual words making up the acronym, it's possible to trigger a series of useful actions to get out of the crisis. Let's examine them together. *Facts*: first of all, we must be able to clearly and objectively identify what is happening, and in order to do this it's necessary to sift the information by separating facts from ideas or impressions, strictly adhering to the here and now, to the 'tangible' reality and not the mental one. In this case a comparison with another person is often useful, if not essential: if there is no agreement on what is happening, it may be that we have misinterpreted the problem, and therefore there is little hope of being able to solve it. We should have the opportunity to verify the information available without being carried away by emotions: it has been amply demonstrated how useful they are, and ultimately fundamental, in the decision-making process, but it is also true that they must not become the protagonists of our choices. The commander of our personal aircraft must remain our 'critical conscience': emotions are just one of the available resources. In recent years, the global attention to the relationship between individuals and their emotional part has been increasing, and different types of techniques (e.g. mindfulness) that allow to reach a greater degree of emotional awareness and acceptance have successfully spread, thereby improving analytical and decision-making skills. The second point of the acronym is the *Options*: once the problem has been identified, it's necessary to define, in an open and effective way, a detailed picture of the possible lines of action that branch out from the critical event and lead to a solution. *Risks and benefits*: having established the framework of possible options, it is necessary to weigh the pros and cons related to each of them, examining the associated advantages and disadvantages. *Decision*: the previous evaluations should have provided, by now, a sufficiently clear picture of the situation to be able to decide which option to follow among those previously examined. Note that if the assessments of *facts*, *options* and *risk analysis* can be effectively shared between two or more people, the *decision* is generally a *personal* process, and for this very reason, it's very often difficult. Taking responsibility for making a choice is often associated with a feeling of discomfort and emotional states such as the fear of making mistakes or being misjudged by others. Choosing a certain path automatically means discarding others, and not knowing what the outcome of our choice will be can put us in serious embarrassment. *Not deciding*, however, not only does not provide any solution to the problem, but often also contributes to making it worse, as an unresolved situation tends to deteriorate further over time. As for the fear of other people's judgment, it doesn't really make much sense, despite its huge emotional charge: it's very rare that someone else can really know which is the best choice for us. Deciding is an art that it is possible to master only by making decisions, and the sooner one starts doing it wisely, the sooner one learns to use this precious resource, even for issues not strictly related to the professional sphere. *Execution*: after making a decision, a series of actions will have to be implemented that will allow to effectively change the situation and to mitigate or solve the problem. *Review*: this entry is often underestimated, but it's very important. At the end of the whole process it's necessary to verify its effectiveness, being also ready to change the pattern of our actions, if these do not prove to be really useful. This means going back to observing the facts, evaluating the options, risks and benefits, making a further decision and executing it: it means, basically, repeating the procedure, keeping the problem under control until it has been solved and the situation has improved. I'll provide some examples starting from a hypothetical situation in which, during a flight, a problem compromises the normal course of operations; we will then extend the technique to a critical situation relating to a hypothetical professional training course. Let's say we are the commander of a flight between United States and Europe that is flying over the Atlantic Ocean. At a certain point the warning lights come on, an alarm starts to sound and the airplane begins to lose altitude: let's use the *FORDER* procedure to manage the emergency. *Facts*: what happened? What is the current situation? We have resources available: instrument indications, experience and, above all, another person sitting next to us. We read the data that the instrumentation provides, discuss them with the other pilot and agree on the nature of the problem: an engine has broken down. *Options*: what can we do? The plane is losing altitude, the alarms continue to sound, maybe there is traffic around us: first of all we put the aircraft in safety by isolating the damaged engine and limiting the power of the one that is still functioning, in order to ensure the physical integrity of the aircraft and the safety of the passengers on board. Then we give the alarm, informing the air traffic control and the nearest traffics about our situation. At this point, what can we do? What are the options? Depending on the seriousness of the situation and other parameters (weather, fuel availability, passenger health status, etc.) we can think of continuing the flight to destination, of returning to the point of departure, of heading to the nearest airport, of flying to another specific location or even of ditching, if the passengers' cabin were filled with smoke and they could no longer breathe. As pilots we would find ourselves having to evaluate the different possibilities, discussing the risks and benefits for each. If an engine is broken, the passengers are fine and there is no fire or smoke on board, it's unnecessary to immediately attempt landing on water, but it's not advisable to strain the remaining engine by staying too long in the air, as would happen by continuing to the destination or returning to the point of departure: a good idea might be to head to the nearest airport. By checking the weather conditions, however, we discover that a snowstorm is in progress at that airport, and that a landing would be rather risky. We keep evaluating conditions at other airports until we find one with acceptable weather: it may not be the closest, but it does offer the benefit of a safe landing. We then discuss with the colleague and as commander take a *decision*: let's go to that specific airport. We *execute*, putting into action what has been decided: we change course, we notify the air traffic control and the passengers, we inform the flight attendants and we follow the procedures. While we are on our way we carry out a *review* of what we are doing: is everything okay? Is what we decided to do still valid? Does it still make sense? Maybe the snowstorm has reached the airport we are flying to, so we will have to change destination. If the conditions have changed, the course of our actions must also change, otherwise we can continue our course of action until landing: we were able to cope with the failure and return to a safe condition. The same technique can give us a first idea of how to proceed even in front of other types of problems in different situations, this time on solid ground. Suppose we are in the middle of a professional training path that will lead us, through a degree course, to the qualification to carry out the profession of our dreams or the one that, for a series of reasons and motivations, we want to be the work of our life. So far everything has gone quite well: we struggled a little but we succeeded in managing the courses, the lessons, the exams, and therefore we have advanced. At a certain point we (fatally) find ourselves having to face a series of courses relating to subjects that we not only hate, but that are also very complex. The teachers are, moreover, strict and unbearable. We're having problems: the professors do not teach well, we do not understand much of what we study and we waste a lot of time studying topics that we do not like, ending up neglecting the other subjects as well. We try to take the exams but we don't pass them: we try once, twice, but we are unsuccessful. Several of our friends, on the other hand, manage quite well while we remain at the stake. After a few months we lift our heads from the books, we look in the mirror and ask ourselves if there is something wrong with what we're doing: maybe it's the whole path we are facing, or maybe there is something wrong with us. Maybe we didn't quite understand what was in store when we chose that degree course. Maybe that kind of work is not really good for us or, in any case, if we have to make such an effort maybe it's better to let it go. What to do? Let's try to use the same kind of *FORDER* technique as we did before and see if it can work. *Facts*: we are in crisis and we can't pass the exams, we are stuck, we feel incompetent and the sight of books makes us feel sick. Okay, and then? Are there any other facts that we can identify, apart from those that directly affect us from an emotional point of view? We can remember that we have already successfully completed part of our professional training path and that, out of the thirty subjects of the course, there are basically only five that we really don't like, and that even at high school we had some problems during the school years, but in the end we managed to pass the final exam in a great way. Furthermore, even if we see that many of our classmates do not have difficulty with the subjects we struggle with, we realize that, unfortunately for them, they have problems in other courses that are not a problem for us at all. We also note that, while it's true that some professors explain badly and are very strict, it's also true that they always stop at the end of the lessons to answer students' questions, trying to clarify the darkest points. Finally, we have many friends who are always willing to talk to us and give us a hand. Perhaps we should have pushed our gaze beyond the barrier of the most negative emotions and include *all the facts, even the positive ones*, in the picture. What is really going on then? We are certainly in trouble and maybe an engine has stopped, but it may also be that we are not exactly crashing. If we begin to suspect that this is the case, how can we verify it? Talking about it with someone and listening to his opinion: this way we would have another evaluation of the available facts that will help us to better frame what is happening. As for the *options*, at a first analysis the choices would basically seem to be only two: we will be able to continue the flight, in this case our path, or abandon and try to land immediately, without reaching the destination, despite the road already traveled. If we start considering the second option, what we can immediately imagine is to perceive at once the relief deriving from the end of the fatigue and stress related to the problem: this is certainly an instant benefit, something that allows us to move away from a situation of crisis that is making us lose time and faith in our abilities. If the benefit of such a choice is immediate, the risk is that its effects will last very little and that more serious problems will take over. Some examples? Having to give up our dreams and our aspirations, not knowing what to put in their place and the feeling that we will have to be content with living a subdued existence compared to our original expectations, perhaps even ending up losing confidence. Let us now consider the first option instead: the risk we perceive is to remain stuck in a condition of stress and frustration which we suffered for nothing, given that our efforts have not been able to get us out of the crisis. However, by exploiting the analysis of the positive facts previously carried out, we can realize that the options available are actually much more: the two immediate possibilities of action (or rather *reaction*) that had flashed into our mind were actually generated, once again, from a limited emotional attitude, perhaps produced by a natural tendency to protect ourselves from noxious stimuli. What more can we think of doing? We can imagine, for example, going to talk to the professors more often, asking questions, asking for explanations and pointing out our difficulties: generally even the most severe teacher appreciates the tenacity, interest and sincerity in a student. We can ask our classmates to give us a hand, since maybe they will be more effective than the professors at simplifying the subjects that are most difficult for us or at illustrating an operating method that they have found useful and decisive. We can balance our feeling of lack of resources with the awareness of the goals we have already achieved during our existence. We can, in a word, look for a different kind of *approach* to the problem, once we find that the one we were using is not working. Instead of changing our path, let's try to *change our behavior*: it may be that we will be able to notice new facts and new available options. In any case it will be necessary to come to a *decision*: continue, look for another route or abandon. Once decided, we will then have to move on to *execution*, implementing the strategy chosen from those considered. Once this is done we will *revise* what we are doing, verifying its effectiveness and evaluating if it's really leading us towards the better condition we were looking for. While the decision is up to us individually, as we ourselves are the commanders of our life, everything else can (and should) be shared with our co-pilots: mates, friends, parents, and so on. Their opinion is also important to allow us to decide for the best. We have so far assumed that we have managed, in one way or another, to make the *right* decision, that is, the one that can take us out of the crisis situation and towards a better condition. What happens, however, if we make a *bad* decision and end up in a worse situation than we were in before? This is actually a rather serious risk, and it's for this reason that a careful analysis must be carried out before choosing, trying not to indulge in what emotions would prompt us to do at once; often this means not giving in to the temptation to immediately eliminate what disturbs us. In fact it has been shown that people who manage to shift the desire for well-being and the need for gratification forward over time, balancing them with the awareness of being able to access greater benefits after overcoming a series of obstacles, enjoy much greater advantages than those who want to 'feel good right away'. Those who manage to achieve their goals find themselves with great confidence in their abilities and can enjoy all the prerogatives that their new condition makes available to them. The advice is therefore to seek refuge in *awareness, tenacity, empathy* and *optimism,* that is, in short, in the resources made available by our *emotional intelligence*: we had put them in our backpack and now the time has come to take them out and use them. The real spring that can continue to push us forward on the road we have taken is the awareness that the game is worth the risk, and that our destination continues to be better than our starting point, for a number of reasons, if we succeed in some way to face the difficulties along the way. In any case, speaking of choices, the advice of others, however precious and fundamental, cannot guarantee the goodness of the decisions that each one must personally make. Making a mistake is a risk: as such, it's possible to minimize it, but it cannot be completely eliminated. While it's true that making mistakes is normal, it's equally true that learning from one's mistakes is often difficult, perhaps even more difficult than learning to choose: we often have a bad relationship with mistakes, we try to hide them, erase them or minimize them; it takes courage to stop and observe them carefully, trying to learn something. It would really be necessary, if we want to improve our ability to make better choices. Let us now return to the evaluation of the options relating to the obstacle that we had considered: one of the possibilities was to let go, stop and abandon. We have already analyzed the reasons why, often, this is not the best option, but it cannot be denied that sometimes we have to recognize that, taking everything into account, it's in fact the only possible choice. What happens in this case? What are the risks and how should we behave? I believe that the greatest risk is that of judging ourselves badly and of losing confidence in ourselves and in our possibilities: while it's normal for this to happen, it's also true that, if we have been honest, we must not be too hard on ourselves. In this case we could perhaps recognize that the mistake was made long before the moment we ran into the obstacle that blocked us, and the merit was that we were able to identify it as such when we were able to do so. Continuing on a path without meaning, without motivation and without passion is perhaps more harmful than useless, and having the courage to abandon it is already a demonstration of awareness and fortitude. However, it is a possibility that can affect everyone and happen at every level of our life, professional and otherwise. In the next chapter we will have the opportunity to evaluate the case of those who discover an error of assessment when they have already achieved their goal. For now I would like to analyze some aspects that arise immediately from the analysis of the problems related to abandoning a professional path. The first is that one might find itself wondering 'what's the point of everything I've done so far?'. We believed we had possibilities, gifts, a purpose, and instead everything suddenly seems to disappear behind a curtain that hides a nebulous reality that we feel bigger than we are. What is the meaning of this type of experience, if there is one? What is waiting for us now? First of all the journey we have made has given us the opportunity to get to know ourselves better and to discover new parts of us that, perhaps, we would never have known if we had not got involved. We had the opportunity to test ourselves and develop skills that, like muscles, had to be stimulated in order to emerge: we will certainly have the opportunity to use them on countless occasions throughout our lives. We have better understood how to make our choices, learning from our mistakes and understanding what are the limits beyond which we are really not willing to go. Perhaps we have also learned *to lose*: this does not mean devoting ourselves to always be defeated, but to experience that even when things go wrong it's possible to recover, to find new strength and motivation and to continue, maybe on another path. Being able to lose without feeling totally defeated is an enormous resource for our existence. We can also note that losing a battle does not mean losing the entire war, and that beyond the despair of the moment the road continues, perhaps in another direction, towards the same goal or a towards a new one. The important thing is that we continue to have a purpose, and in this sense it is essential to build a plan B, a secondary road, an emergency exit that would allow us to continue dreaming and aiming for a new life that contains the seeds of a better existence. It's a great skill, and many of the more successful people, such as captains of industry, innovative startuppers, movie stars or successful entrepreneurs are such precisely because they had one or more backup plans that went into operation when they realized that the road they were traveling on was not really theirs. Sometimes we only realize *in retrospect* the significance of our failures and the opportunities they have opened up for us. Let us remember, for example, Steve Jobs, founder of Apple, one of the most successful industries on the planet, who was able to gather the strings of many interrupted study and work experiences and to merge them into a new, exciting project that characterized the rest of his life. The secret, and we will talk about it shortly, is *to be aware* that everything that happens to us, *including failures*, can be seen as a *source of new opportunities*. We must remain *open* and *receptive*, and not closed in a private space made of self-pity. Obstacles, although inevitable, are a gym where we can train and develop our qualities, making new ones emerge. They provide us with opportunities to better understand who we are and what we can do, opening doors to new ways of realizing ourselves that we never even imagined.

CHAPTER FIVE: VISIONS FROM ABOVE

We have dealt with how to identify a path that can lead to our dream job through a personal analysis focused on desires, attitudes, abilities and willingness to commit ourselves to achieving our goals. We have so far addressed an audience that includes, above all, those who are facing the problem of choosing their profession, such as high school students. I would now like to broaden the discussion by adding other points of view, which can integrate what has already been discussed regarding the methods that allow us to finalize our projects, and by including other people in the analysis, such as those who *already have a job* but who, for some reason, are not satisfied with it and see themselves far from their professional achievement goals. We can think of the kind of approach proposed so far as a classic pattern of *Western* thought: *get busy*. If I want to achieve something or become someone, I have to commit, I have to act. This concept is true and it works, in most cases: we just have to be convinced that the distance that separates us from our desires can almost always be effectively covered through an appropriate course of action. However there is also another school of thought that provides a different type of approach to the problem, including the question of one's own personal or professional fulfillment: the *Eastern* one. In this case the way of dealing with the question is different from what we just described: the emphasis is not so much on what we can do to *achieve* a goal, but on how *aware* we are of the *opportunities* that life offers us, including, of course, the professional ones. I find this attitude very interesting and I think it can be effectively integrated into any type of path that we may find ourselves considering. In addition to understanding how we are really made, what we really want and to commit ourselves to achieve our goals, sometimes it would be really appropriate to become aware of what is happening around us and what reality already makes available to us: perhaps what we are looking for it's closer than we can imagine, and we don't notice it because we are too busy with the realization of our own private project. Maybe it would be enough to look around to recognize that life already presents us with opportunities. That said, I would like to clarify that I am not saying that to make our dreams come true it is enough wait for the universe to drop what we are looking for on our open hand: it doesn't work like this. What I mean is that, since our existence is something much larger and more complex than our ideas, it can be useful to look around us in an open and inclusive way, so as not to miss out on possible opportunities just because they don't fit into the detailed pattern we have drawn in our mind. How many times have we heard that to be fulfilled in life it is also necessary to have *luck*? It is true, but luck is, in this case, to be understood as the ability to notice something useful that happens along the path we have undertaken and to include it in our project. If we go on blindfolded, it will be very difficult for luck to give us a hand. Realizing what beauty the universe can give us is essential to develop a sense of *gratitude* towards life experiences in general: this can allow us to better appreciate whatever may happen to us before judging it useless, unpleasant or even harmful. Being grateful means living better and, consequently, studying or working better, allowing ourselves to notice the positive sides of things and developing a more complete ability to evaluate our life and our condition, including the professional one. This doesn't mean, of course, enjoying any situation or uncritically accepting every job opportunity that opens up in front of us: it's important to continue to be guided by our dreams and desires, but we must be aware that, since we're unable to see with certainty the road in front of us, often we are not able to fully understand the meaning that what we are experiencing in this moment may have someday. Sometimes we only understand in retrospect the importance that what seemed unwelcome had on what we later came to build. Having an inclusive attitude can therefore help us in this way, allowing us not to miss the chance to recognize these hidden opportunities. Now, let's take a few steps forward and imagine that we have finally reached the end of our professional journey and now we can do the job of our dreams: we will certainly, and rightly, be more than satisfied with what we have managed to do, we have increased our confidence in our skills and we have acquired an operating method that, perhaps with some variations, we will be able to use again for the new challenges that will open up to us. *New challenges?* Aren't they finished yet? It's said that exams never end, and in fact the end of a professional training path does not necessarily coincide with the end of our efforts: indeed, in many ways, it's right *after* that moment that we really need to get involved and learn how to work. The information and the basics learned along the formative journey are used and applied specifically to the type of work we're going to do. We have to take a good leap, *but now we know who we are, what we can do and how we can do it.* These three assumptions, and all that they contain (from personal qualities, to the resources of emotional intelligence, to the awareness of previous experiences), are the most precious legacy that our training will have given us. We can rely on them to take the first steps into the wider labour market. Beginning a new profession one discovers a new landscape, generally a little different from the imagined one: it can be better or worse than we expected. If what we are facing is good, then the situation is certainly ideal! In this case we were able to use our *awareness*, truly coming to fully enjoy all that our new experience can offer us. It can also happen, however, that what we are facing is much worse than what we hoped to find after all the hard work. I lived this experience firsthand: after graduation, the jobs that I initially found were very different not only from what I had wanted, but also from what I had simply imagined. It's not a good feeling: you start to fear that you have worked so hard just to get to something you want to immediately escape from, fearing to be entangled in a condition that you do not like and that you are not willing to accept. Of course this does not necessarily happen, but it can. It's a disappointing and distressing experience: we wonder if we'll be forced to abdicate our dreams and have to accept to live with a profession that, despite our best efforts, is not good for us.

What to do? First of all, do not panic: our condition is now very different from the one we started from. *We took a path, learned something and trained. We are no longer the same persons* who started walking the uncertain path to their dreams years ago: we have developed other skills, we have matured, we have understood how to deal with problems, we have a *method*. In addition to all this, we can also be *aware* to the reality that surrounds us and identify possible ways out that, perhaps, are already available. We can also use *gratitude* to treasure what we live, because it carries a hidden meaning that will later prove precious. Maybe we also have a *plan B*, that will allow us to take another direction which, although not exactly coinciding with the one planned, will certainly be better than the one we ended up in. Having already reached a goal, therefore, provides us with new resources that we can use together with those already present in our backpack to improve the quality of our life. What should never be forgotten is that *it's always possible to change*: however difficult it may seem, there is the possibility of abandoning a path that we don't like, and set out for a better one. It can be hard, but it can be done: I think the hardest thing is to decide to do it. Even in the case of a change of profession, the already described *FORDER* technique can be used advantageously, providing us with a guide through the decision-making process with all the precautions discussed before. Of course it may be that the prospect of having to struggle again when you were convinced that you have already arrived at your destination may not be particularly appealing, but what will really make the difference, pushing us to act, will be how we perceive the quality of our life: as long as we will consider it acceptable we will be able to continue doing the same job, but if this is not the case we will naturally be pushed to do something, deciding whether the game is worth the risk or not. On the other hand there are people for whom changing job is almost a necessity: they hardly feel fulfilled and continue to chase always different or more articulated dreams. This can become a real drug: their motivation is *challenge* and their goals, consequently, are never enough. These people need to go further and further and reach increasingly complex, important and demanding positions. This can be very stimulating, but it comes with a risk: losing much of the rest of one's life. Work is, for each of us, a very important part of existence and often the one that requires most of our time. We must not forget, however, that there are also other things that contribute to personal realization, equally important and necessary for the construction of our happiness. We should be able to balance each of the parts we need in our life (work, family, free time) so as not to end up hostage to any of them in particular, enjoying instead what each can offer. The success and satisfactions that our profession can give us, especially if it is the one of our dreams, can become drugs and, as such, they end up producing unwanted effects, the consequences of which often show up only after a long time. There are many who, perhaps unwittingly, find themselves living their work without caring about anything else. The risk is that all other aspects of life loose their importance. Quite a few people notice this trap and try to do something that can bring a new balance in their life; these are often individuals who are initially very motivated and dedicated to very complex and demanding professions: they struggled to reach those positions, they wanted it and they spent lots and lots of energies to get there. One day, however, they became aware not only of the effort and commitment required by their difficult jobs, but also of the way in which they committed themselves to it. Some of them, after thinking about it, decided to change direction, turning to less complex professions or changing their way of relating to their work, thus managing to access those aspects of their lives that they had previously neglected and which had become important in the meantime. Generally the most common choice is to change job and do something different (possibly something creative) that leaves the possibility to decide how much to dedicate to what you do. A dear friend of mine, after graduating in engineering management, had embarked on a dazzling career as a manager for some large international groups. She traveled a lot, she often lived abroad, she was payed very well, she was always busy and her contribution was recognized by everyone as fundamental. She continued to live like this for years, until she realized that all this was going to invalidate another deep desire of hers: to have a family. It took her some time, but she finally decided to take another direction and, after the birth of her daughter, she left her job and dedicated herself to the design and manufacture of handcrafted jewelry, something that she liked and that at the same time allowed her to better manage her time and to be with her family. It should be noted that she managed to implement a plan B which, however, was *one of her dreams*, perhaps even the most intimate and personal. It may be that she hadn't initially thought of being able to do it right away, and therefore embarked on another path of professional formation that interested her anyway, even if it was perhaps a little less fascinating. In any case it was by dedicating herself to it and discovering its limits that she had the opportunity to realize an even greater dream, her *true dream*. As we can see, we can reach our dreams also in a progressive way, step by step, and our efforts are never lost, in fact they contribute to bringing out other qualities and resources that will allow us to push ourselves even further, to believe in ourselves and to feel capable of being able to realize even what seems furthest from our daily reality. The more we challenge ourselves and train, the more we can afford to forget what we have to do and to devote ourselves with gusto to what we want to do. However every journey, even the longest, begins with a small step: however tiny it may be, that step is still necessary.

CHAPTER SIX: DEBRIEFING

I wanted to entitle this last chapter with the technical term used to indicate the moment in which, after the flight, once the plane is parked, the engines switched off, the on-board documents completed and the passengers disembarked, the pilots sum up what they have done, criticizing in an open and constructive way how they have carried out their mission. It's a very important phase of their work, in which everyone can learn something from the analysis of the operations. We too have somehow made a flight over a landscape made up of many arguments, insights and reflections and, like the pilots, we can now try to draw conclusions. Since I am in the privileged position of the one who is physically putting his ideas and reflections on paper, I will start the *debriefing*, knowing that it will remain incomplete until the readers also have contributed their own part, which I urge them to do once the last page is turned. First of all a brief summary: starting from the experiences that the author lived to get to the job he dreamed of, we began to identify the reasons that can guide us towards certain professional goals (*passions* and *motivations*), analyzing the weight of each of them in the choice of a specific path. We then took care of defining the tools that can effectively accompany us to our goal, identifying the most important ones and the role they play. We then talked about *obstacles* and difficulties, and how they can become *opportunities* for change and for confrontation with ourselves. We continued with the importance of an *open*, *curious* and *positive* attitude towards the experiences that we may find ourselves living during and after the professional training, taking into account that even when we begin to practice our profession we will have to continue learning and that, in any case, what has been done previously will have made available new methods and tools that we can use in our work and in our life. Finally we mentioned that, apart from our professional growth, our commitment has also the credit of giving us a personal one, and the person we see in the mirror at the end of the path, however it went, will be better than the one we used to see before. Now, can we perhaps draw some conclusions? I would say yes, and many in my opinion. The first is that *our passions and our motivations are important*, whatever they may be: they certainly don't have to invade every corner of our life, but they are very powerful engines to move forward, grow and be happy. Realizing one's passions certainly has a great positive or negative influence on us and on our way of being. There are people who consider their dreams unattainable or who even think they are not up to their aspirations, taking refuge in the most tested and safe schemes offered by the collective culture through the media and social networks: do not fall into this trap. Each of us deserves to be able to express what he is and what he carries within himself through his work: it's like being an artist who speaks about himself through his works, and I would like to remind you that all the professions in the Middle Ages were considered as *arts. Be the artists of yourselves and of your life: take yourselves seriously, get involved and make it a masterpiece.* You can do it, you just have to want to. Difficult? Yes. Impossible? No. "Impossible is nothing", used to say Cassius Clay, an African-American boxer who, going through the difficulties of a troubled life, managed to become World Champion: here's a person who has overcome incredible obstacles becoming, moreover, famous and successful. It's not by avoiding difficulties that you end up feeling better: they will recur all the same, in another way. We might as well face them to improve our lives. James Baldwin, an American writer, used to say that "not everything we face can be changed, but nothing can be changed if we don't face it": we can never completely eliminate the uncertainty about the outcome of our efforts, but only by addressing it we may have a chance to accomplish something. Let's follow our dreams and what we truly feel, however unusual they may be, rather than adjusting to mass standards that tend to produce a flat and predictable society: differences, new ideas and innovations are what make this world interesting, and if many will tell you that you are crazy to abandon the safety of a straight and safe path for a narrower and more winding one, you will probably be on the right path, if you approach it with commitment and seriousness. Speaking of this, I would like to recommend a beautiful film that tells the story of a child in England in the eighties, the son of a miner in financial straits, who has a very particular passion that contrasts with the world that surrounds him and the life he leads. Its title is 'Billy El-liott': I won't tell you anything else, watch it because it's really worth it. Whatever the goal we want to achieve, we have to try. American astronaut Terry Virts, commander of the International Space Station who spent seven months in orbit around the Earth, says that from a very young age he had a passion for flying and a desire to go to space. When he told his family about it, they just smiled at him and considered his ideas as the somewhat bizarre ravings of a child. Moving forward with his life, Terry never abandoned his dreams and began to draw up concrete projects to reach his goals: colleges, scientific universities, military aviation. After many years, he obtained the necessary qualifications to be able to participate in selections for NASA. Terry says he knew it was going to be extremely difficult to succeed, but that *if he didn't try he was sure he wouldn't have any chance of succeeding.* So how did he do it? '*I went to the selections and I tried to do my best*', he says, '*without pre-conceptions or prejudices*'. Here's the words of a man who has fully lived his dream. He had to work, he didn't know if he would have succeeded, but *he tried doing his best* and, guess what, *he succeeded.* Perhaps the most difficult thing is to believe that it's possible to bring one's dreams to earth, that dreams are not only fascinating but evanescent ideas around our brain: we must believe that they are *legitimate, achievable, possible,* and that one day we will be able to *live* them. The possibility exists, it's up to us to take the first step and do the best we can. If we don't decide to move, we can be sure that we will never get there; if we do, this possibility exists. What hinders many people is not having enough self-esteem, not trusting their abilities, being afraid of failing: it's important to be able to look at ourselves with a different view, and not to set presumed limits that maybe don't even exist at all. If we really want to discover what we can do we must *try*, maybe not just once, but two, three, fifty or a hundred times: *tenacity* is one of the most important qualities of emotional intelligence. Many successful people (for example, the writer JK Rowlings, the author of the Harry Potter saga, or the actor Brad Pitt, or the astronaut Paolo Nespoli) had to go through years of rejections, negative judgments and secondary roles before having the opportunity to break through. But *they never gave up*. Let us not be discouraged: the point is not to see ourselves as powerful, infallible or invincible, but only to feel entitled *to believe* in what we do and to get used to thinking that *we can do it*. It's important to have this attitude, without leading to immodesty or even arrogance, but simply doing our best because *we have something to give and we can make a difference*. No one is a useless spectator: each one of us can give his own precious contribution to the construction of the world and the society, and can do so by realizing and expressing himself through his work. Let's not be too influenced by the 'culture' of the moment: let's be trend setters ourselves, people who define models and ways of life that fascinate and that others can decide to follow. If we are enthusiastic about our dreams and we manage to materialize them, we will also be able to share them with others, and perhaps many will tell us 'what you do has inspired me too'. Speaking of sharing and interdependence between people, naturally one ends up talking about *team work*. Beyond the methodologies that can allow an optimization of the collaboration between those who work in a group, one of the most illuminating experiences is to discover that what we know can integrate effectively with what others know, producing results far greater than those we would have obtained by working alone. In other words a group of people who work well together can produce greater results than the sum of the contributions that any single person can provide. Whatever our dream job is, remember that it will most likely have to include a collaboration and it won't remain some sort of private engagement. Other people are necessary for the realization of our dreams and *learning to cooperate is essential*. Professional training is not only a solitary effort in which everyone is committed as much as possible to achieve his own goals: it must also develop our ability to relate correctly and effectively, in order to lay the foundations of what one day will become our daily team work. Unfortunately, during training, the emphasis on this aspect is usually not often enough: it's only after starting to work that we can have some information about it. However we can get used to a comparison with the others by trying to communicate clearly and effectively, listening and reflecting before proposing our ideas, remaining available to other people's proposals and not being afraid to change our mind if someone else had a better idea. It's also important to learn to defend our own ideas and positions from the destructive criticism that inevitably, sooner or later, someone will give us, perhaps with a friendly expression and a smile on their lips. It's therefore a skill that must be learned, and if no one has taught us yet it will be necessary to develop it ourselves. Knowing how to work in a team is essential: let's get used to consider it as a quality to be cultivated with great attention. *Courage* is also an aspect not to be overlooked, a sort of backbone that runs through and supports our entire professional journey, from the beginning to the end. It's the necessary condition to start our journey, to move forward and to get up when we fall; it's what really allows us to start over every time something frustrates our efforts. Like many other qualities, it functions like a muscle, and it must be strengthened through *use*. Being courageous doesn't mean not having fears or throwing ourselves into whatever goes through our mind, but rather being able to focus on the present moment without being diverted by the strength of our negative emotions. If we are following a path, we will often have fears or doubts due to the fact that we do not know what awaits us or how we can overcome an obstacle: well, let's accept the reality of having these uncertainties and move on. Reality is almost always different from the movie that our emotional side offers to distract us from taking risks, and it's precisely those who manage to bring out their courage in these moments and continue on their journey who, in the end, manage to reach the goal. Our emotions are certainly strong and important, but *they do not define us. We are not what we feel but what we choose to do.* We must have the strength not to identify ourselves with our fears but to feel them, accept them and go beyond them. Each of us can also find an antidote to use as a remedy for emotional difficulties experienced at certain times. Personally, when I found myself in critical, difficult or uncertain conditions, being assailed by the fear of not making it, I found that forcing myself to have a good laugh was of great help: it may seem absurd to laugh when facing a difficult situation or when things have already gone wrong and one doesn't know what to do, but, as far as I'm concerned, this simple action has always managed to change my psychological perspective, reducing the importance and weight of what was happening and somehow bringing back to my attention all the other resources that enriched my life. This is my experience: it's up to you to find a way to stigmatize your courage and the will to challenge the adversities of the moment with an appropriate gesture. We must always remember, or at least suspect, even when we feel defeated by events, that we are bigger and stronger than our problems and overcoming them is not a question of ability, but only of time: if we hold on we will make it. Furthermore, since it's impossible to separate the realization of our dreams from our life and that a professional growth also corresponds to a personal one, it's inevitable that sooner or later the quality of our life will also influence that of our training or our work. It's not possible to live in watertight compartments, and the different aspects of our existence are closely linked to each other: to succeed in what we do, we must also make sure that the rest of our life makes us feel good. Studying and working take up a large part of our day, and the reason is clear to us if we are following our projects, but we must not allow them to completely invade our time. Daily commitment gives great meaning to our existence, but rest, leisure, friendships, sports, hobbies allow us to recover from fatigue and be even more effective when we return to our occupations. As far as my personal experience goes, studying is also an important part of the pilot's work: procedures, regulations, operations change all the time, and it's always necessary to stay informed and up to date. Twice a year, moreover, for two consecutive days at a time, we go to the simulator, a machine that exactly reproduces the cockpit and which, as the name implies, is able to simulate every condition which the plane can meet during the flight, with movements, sounds and even smoke. The main purpose is to train pilots to deal with the main failures or situations that have led to various accidents, but it's also used to *check* that the pilots know how to do their job, faithfully following the procedures, performing the various maneuvers in a correct manner and managing emergencies effectively. It's a sort of particular and very long class assignment, given that briefing, session and debriefing take about seven hours. It's a fairly complex and tiring experience, also because it often takes place at night, and it's obviously necessary to prepare a lot to be able to pass the exam. Once an instructor commander I was staying with in a hotel, who was supposed to be examining my colleague and me during the simulator session at night, saw me in the late afternoon sitting at a table studying in a lounge near the lobby. He came over, patted me on the shoulder and said, 'Don't study all day! You'll have to work hard tonight and your body and mind need rest: it's better to study less and rest more'. I looked at him, smiled, got up, picked up my books and went to my room to rest. Everything went well that night, and from that moment I realized that often, in the past, I had continued to revise despite having already studied everything, trying to satisfy my fear of failure and completely forgetting the most basic needs of my body, such as eating or resting. Everyone happens to have to work overtime: it's normal. This, however, must not become a habit because this way of acting can lead to situations of psychophysical stress that can lead to failure of the tests instead of increasing performance, and it's therefore essential to develop the ability to balance effort and commitment with rest and recreation. Even today, when I find myself busy with pressing commitments, when I have to prepare myself for an exam, a check or when I have a lot to do, I never forget the advice that commander gave me and, first of all, I try to organize myself so that the time devoted to preparation is adequate, leaving room for rest and distraction. Allocating twenty-four hours a day to getting ready can ultimately lead to a lower performance than hoped for: even the machines do not always work at maximum power. Take it easy: you can make a serious commitment without forgetting the rest of your life. What we need to do is bring *quality* into our commitment, concentrating and immersing ourselves effectively in what we are doing, whether it be working or studying, without filling all our time with a minimal effort. A question that someone may ask is: 'When I finally reach my destination and I'm finally doing my dream job, what will my life be like? I will be satisfied, I will be busy, I will be different: but will my dreams end there?'. Of course not: one of the good things in life is that dreams never end. We can fulfill one and discover that there are a thousand others waiting for us around the corner. They will not be identical and will concern different aspects of our existence: many of them will not even be exclusively our dreams, but will be shared and realized with someone else. Perhaps the latter will be the most complex, most beautiful and greatest dreams that we will find ourselves trying to realize. Our whole life is in fact the realization of our different dreams, each of which will integrate with the others as pieces of a mosaic that, in the end, will form a beautiful design, the one that will represent what we want our existence to be. Someone said that 'the things we pay attention to end up becoming our life': let's try then to pay attention to our dreams, which are often beautiful and are the truest part of us, so that they end up becoming our everyday reality. The more we take them seriously, as something achievable, the more we will be willing to invest in them and to justify the efforts necessary to make them happen. If realizing a dream can be difficult, it's also true that a life without dreams is flat and dull: it is precisely trying, getting involved and committing oneself that in the end give us back taste, meaning and satisfaction, that make us say 'it was hard, but I made it', that make us think of other possibilities that can allow us to look at ourselves in the mirror with a smile of appreciation. It's certainly wrong to judge people on the basis of what they are able or unable to do, but it's true that what we do is important and speaks about us to ourselves and to the world. After all a great dream is never something private and exclusive: in some way it will always end up interacting with others and with their life, perhaps improving it. Let's be aware and confident that the *vocation* that emerges from everyone's dream will not only have meaning for us, but will also give more meaning to the world, mysteriously meshing with the dreams and vocations of others to form an even greater and admirable mosaic: that's why I believe that trying to really make someone's dreams come true can somehow make the world better. Dreaming is something serious and must be taken seriously, also because if our true desires remain unfulfilled, they will sooner or later come knocking on our door asking for our attention. Since we cannot silence them or eliminate them, we will therefore have to deal with them sooner or later: it's better to do it as soon as possible! The fact of succeeding or not, always remains an unknown factor: the risk of not achieving what one was committed to really exists. There are however several aspects that we must not forget. The first is that, beyond the fact of reaching our goal or not (and if you remember, we said that with a serious commitment this is *very* likely), we are giving our existence a meaning and we can feel involved, motivated, with a purpose: in a word, we can feel *alive*. It's an incomparable sensation, and sometimes it happens in life, perhaps during a moment of boredom or absolute tranquility, when nothing complicated comes to disturb the calm of a flat day, to be thinking with a smile about that time when, after a lot of effort, we managed to do what we wanted. Even the effort then seems to be something pleasant, a sort of *challenge* against a series of difficulties in which, in the end, one managed to win. By dint of getting involved, overcoming obstacles and hitting goals, the desire to try new experiences also increases, and life is enriched with many new possibilities when you come to understand that *you can succeed in anything*, if you commit yourself. One feels capable of opening new doors and less willing to accept a condition uncritically, wondering instead how to improve it. Life then becomes an exciting adventure, made up of discoveries and difficult but certainly pleasant challenges. It's like a good football match: you know that you will have to work hard to win, the result can hang by a thread until the very end, but you can't wait to play and, when you do it, you do it with passion. When the game ends you talk about it with enthusiasm, if you have won, and can't wait to play again to win, if you have lost: what will not change will be *the desire to get back into the game*. Let's keep this feeling close: it's an important part of our existence and it's precisely what can make us enjoy even the biggest efforts that we made. A second fact is that, if we don't immediately hit our target, we can ask ourselves questions about *how* we are acting and adjusting the shot, changing methods. I have noticed that often, to be able to hit the mark, aiming at the center of the target is not enough: one has to aim a little higher. In this way, even if we fail to conquer that extra piece that we have added to our purposes, we will most likely be able to achieve our original goal. How can we aim a little higher? We must try to give a little more and, above all, slightly modify our *expectations* regarding what we are doing, always maintaining a balance between the effort made and the need to rest and relax. It's not easy: one needs to be capable of an almost painstaking organization and an iron will, but certainly we can try. The risk, in this case, is to end up becoming very critical of oneself and one's commitment, so I recommend it only to very balanced people who little inclined to judge themselves. However, it is a strategy that can be used by everyone, at least in principle, as long as you do not overdo the demands on your *performance* capabilities. What we do to build our dreams builds ourselves, improving ourselves, bringing out our qualities and equipping ourselves with new skills. It's never wasted time, not even in the (remote) case in which we fail to reach the destination we set ourselves: if we haven't found the job of our dreams, we can probably realize that we have found *our true selves*, or at least someone we like very much and who comes very close to it. This may be unexpected, a sort of *collateral effect* produced by what we have accomplished along our path, and it's undoubtedly one of the most important aspects that our experience gives us back. It's a gift that is given to us, whatever the outcome of our efforts may be, so let's try to be aware of its presence and its importance, which is often also decisive for the other experiences that we will have to make in the course of our life. We said that luck is the ability to notice what is useful along the way and to include it in our life project: never as in this case can we say that having embarked on the path towards our dreams has allowed us to acquire new aspects of ourselves that are just waiting to be discovered, and that can be used profitably during our existence. The last topic that I would like to discuss concerns the mysterious attention that the universe shows towards those who have decided to take a certain path. A saying also cited by Samantha Cristoforetti, the Italian astronaut, says: 'the world moves to let pass those who know where to go'. It's just like that: somehow, our will, our optimism, our dedication and our conviction are transmitted to the world which, in turn, collaborates with our intentions, making events happen that lead us towards our own destination. Perhaps this is due to the fact that when we are truly convinced of what we do, we are also more attentive to what surrounds us and more predisposed to seize opportunities. Of course this doesn't happen always but only on the few occasions when we are totally immersed in some activity that deeply involves us and about which we have no doubts. But then where is the universe when you work hard and you don't get where you wanted? Why didn't he give us a hand just when we needed it? Why did he not want to share our desires and contribute to their realization? The best of the answers is found in a phrase from a beautiful song by the Rolling Stones: *'You can't always get what you want, but if you try sometimes you may get what you need'*. Life and the universe never abandon us, and keep on conspiring with us more than we can think, leading us to discover that what we were really looking for was something we never even imagined. But, as the song says, we have *to try*: if we try, we will never be truly disappointed. Let's start the journey and we will arrive at a destination: it will almost certainly be the one we want and, if not, we will still be able to discover that we have reached a beautiful new landing place full of surprises. 'Life is the realization of the dream of youth, and man wishes, by his nature, to be the protagonist', said Karol Wojtyla: let's keep dreaming and we will never stop enjoying life and all that it has to offer.

CHAPTER SEVEN: SOME WORDS
FROM THE CHAMPIONS

Before saying goodbye and leaving you to think, I would like to add to my testimony that of many people who have managed to see their dreams come true after putting themselves on the line, having struggled in the face of uncertainties and difficulties. They are famous and often successful individuals coming from various fields: from sports, to science, to philosophy, politics, art, entrepreneurship, fashion, music, cinema. It's not important what they do or did, but how they managed to get where they wanted to. They have three aspects in common: the fact of believing in their dreams, the courage to try to make them come true and that of not having given up when facing challenges, hardships and adversities. Their path has often been very long, uncertain and difficult, but they have reached the goal and, above all, they have become everything they could be. They clashed with fears, doubts and failures, but this was not enough to erase the tenacity and determination along the road that led to their dreams, and their advice is certainly precious. Therefore, here are some words from those who made it.

- *If you can dream it, you can do it.* W. Disney, American artist

- *The most difficult thing is the decision to act, the rest is merely tenacity.* A Earhart, American aviator

- *A winner is a dreamer who newer gives up.* N. Mandela, South African politician and Nobel Prize winner

- *It's the possibility of having a dream come true that makes life interesting.* P. Coelho, Portuguese writer

- *The best preparation for tomorrow is doing your best today.* H.J. Brown, American writer

- *There is no favorable wind for the sailor who does not know where to go.* Seneca, Latin philosopher and writer

- *Choose a job you love and you'll never have to work a day in your life.* Confucius, Chinese philosopher

- *You can't be afraid to fail, it's the only way you succeed.* L. James, American NBA superstar

- *Don't be afraid of difficult times: the best comes from there.* R. Levi Montalcini, Italian geneticist and Nobel Prize winner

- *When everything seems to be going against you, remember that the airplane takes off against the wind, not with it.* H. Ford, American industrialist

- *There are only two mistakes one can make along the road to truth: not going all the way, and not beginning.* Buddha, Indian philosopher

- *Believe you can and you're halfway there.* T. Roosevelt, president of the U.S.A.

- *It is never too late to be what you might have been.* G. Eliot, British writer

- *Too many of us are not living our dreams because we are living our fears.* L. Brown, American journalist and opinion leader

- *The biggest risk is not taking any risk.* M. Zuckerberg, creator of Facebook

- *Courage is like a muscle: we strengthen it with use.* R. Gordon, American actress.

- *Everybody knows that something can't be done and then somebody turns up and he doesn't know it can't be done and he does it.* A. Einstein, scientist and Noble Prize winner

- *You don't learn to walk by following rules. You learn by doing, and by falling over.* R. Branson, British entrepreneur

- *A man is a success if he gets up in the morning and gets to bed at night, and in between he does what he wants to do.* Bob Dylan, American songwriter

- *They told me I could not do it, that's why I did it!* A. Schwarzenegger, American actor

- *Do not give up! You would risk doing it an hour before the miracle.* Arabic saying

- *Be always like the sea, than breaking up against cliffs it finds always the force to try again.* Jim Morrison, American rockstar and poet

- *I can accept failure, everyone fails at something. But I can't accept not trying.* M. Jordan, American NBA superstar

- *Those who fear failure do not move.* Orazio, Latin poet and writer

- *People should pursue what they're passionate about. That will make them happier than pretty much anything else.* E. Musk, American entrepreneur

- *No matter who you are, no matter what you did, no matter where you've come from, you can always change, become a better version of yourself.* Madonna, American rockstar

- *If you want something you've never had you have to do something you've never done.* T. Jefferson, founding father and president of the U.S.A.

- *The harder the victory, the greater the happiness in winning.* Pelé, Brasilian soccer legend

- *If you hear a voice within you say 'you cannot paint', then by all means paint and that voice will be silenced.* V. Van Gogh, Dutch painter

- *You don't become what you want, you become what you believe.* O. Winfrey, American TV star and actress

- *Don't make choices because somebody else is telling you it's good from a career perspective.* B. Pitt, American actor

- *When you cease to dream you cease to live.* M. Forbes, American editor

- *Fall seven times, get up eight.* Japanese saying

- *As for the future, it is not a question of predicting it but of making it possible.* A. De Saint-Exupery, French writer and aviator

- *Success is not final, failure is not fatal: it is the courage to continue that counts.* W. Churchill, British statesman

- *A man is but the product of his thoughts. What he thinks, he becomes.* M. Gandhi, Indian statesman

- *Your time is limited, so don't waste it living someone else's life. Don't be trapped by dogma - which is living with the results of other people's thinking. Don't let the noise of other's opinions drown out your own inner voice. And most important, have the courage to follow your heart and intuition. They somehow already know what you truly want to become. Everything else is secondary... Stay hun-*

gry, stay foolish. Steve Jobs, founder of Apple

www.ingramcontent.com/pod-product-compliance
Lightning Source LLC
Chambersburg PA
CBHW060912130726
48001CB00006B/2209